RETIREMENT INCOME CHOICES 101

Michael Corbett

CONTENTS

RETIREMENT INCOME CHOICES 101

This book is supported by free software and video available at www.MyRetirementLibrary.com. Online features include the following:

SEGMENT ONE

TRAINING VIDEO:
PERIODIC WITHDRAWAL (11:32 MIN)

INTERACTIVE SOFTWARE:
PERIODIC WITHDRAWAL GRAPHING CALCULATOR

SEGMENT TWO

TRAINING VIDEO:
VARIABLE LIFE ANNUITY (11:04 MIN)

INTERACTIVE SOFTWARE:
ONE ITERATION CALCULATOR
MULTIPLE ITERATIONS CALCULATOR

SEGMENT THREE

TRAINING VIDEO:
MONTE CARLO ANALYSIS (9:56 MIN)

INTERACTIVE SOFTWARE:
TOTAL PROBABILITY PAYOUT CALCULATOR
LONGEVITY FREQUENCY CALCULATOR

FOREWORD

This book is supported by free software and video available at:

MyRetirementLibrary.com

These tools are designed to educate retirees about the two most popular income choices: the **Periodic Withdrawal** and the **Variable Life Annuity**. They each have pros and cons.

The **Periodic Withdrawal** will allow you to maintain complete control of your retirement income, but that also means that you'll be taking on all of the budgetary and investment risk by yourself. On the other hand, purchasing a **Variable Life Annuity** will provide you with reasonable protection from much of the budgetary and market risk, but in exchange you'll take on some mortality risk (i.e. the risk that you'll die prematurely and not get back the full amount you paid into the contract).

If you're considering these choices, this volume will guide you through the analysis needed to determine which is right for your situation. Of course, it is also highly recommended that you seek out the advice of a Financial Planner to talk about your specific circumstances, and employ professional grade analysis software.

PART I

CHAPTER ONE

WHAT IS A PERIODIC WITHDRAWAL?

A **Periodic Withdrawal** is the process of an individual managing their own income during retirement. It involves the individual deciding how to invest the money, how much to withdraw, and when to withdraw it.

This process can also be referred to as a systematic withdrawal, an automated withdrawal, an asset drawdown, or a self-managed withdrawal.

The primary goal of a periodic withdrawal is to preserve assets and maintain flexibility, so that an individual can take as much or as little of their savings as they please.

THE BASIC PERIODIC WITHDRAWAL

The set of assumptions introduced below will illustrate the risks and potential rewards associated with a Periodic Withdrawal. These assumptions will be built upon in later chapters as the examples become more complex.

George is 65 and has $860,000. He's invested the whole amount into a stock fund that he believes will pay an average annual return of 7.5%. He plans to withdraw $60,000 a year to cover his expenses and hopes the income will last for the duration of his lifetime. These assumptions are listed below, and will be entered into a calculator which will generate a set of results.

ASSUMPTIONS

Beginning Balance: $860,000
Return: 7.5%
Withdrawal: $60,000
Life Expectancy: 100

THE RESULTS

As shown in the screenshot below, the assumptions have led to a very stable income stream. The income has lasted to age 100 (the maximum age allowed by the calculator); and the balance has grown fast enough to replenish itself. This income stream will last forever:

This is everyone's dream scenario! Unfortunately, there are two significant problems with this model: **Investment Volatility** and **Inflation** have been left out. In order to build a more realistic model, we must understand these concepts and add them to our model.

ADDITIONAL NOTES ON THE PERIODIC WITHDRAWAL GRAPHING CALCULATOR

On the calculator, the blue bars represent withdrawals while the orange bars represent the balance. If you're viewing a black and white version of these images, the withdrawals will show up as the darker color.

The Y-Axis represents dollars and the X-Axis represents units of time. Time is moving from left to right. When the blue bars disappear, the retirement income has run out. The calculator will model income up to the age of 100, at which point it will report the total amount of money paid out and any remaining balance (which is shown on the calculator below the graph).

3

*Assumptions used in creating the income models in the **Periodic Withdrawal Calculator** are as follows:*

- *Returns are after expenses.*
- *Taxes are not considered.*
- *Withdrawals are made at the beginning of the period.*

CONCLUSION

A retirement model must take into account **Investment Volatility** and **Inflation**, in order to produce meaningful results. The next few chapters will explain these two concepts and then integrate them into the **Periodic Withdrawal Model**.

CHAPTER ONE QUESTIONS

1.) What is a Periodic Withdrawal?

    A.) The systematic withdrawal of funds to cover your living expenses.

    B.) Withdrawals of a set amount made at predetermined intervals.

    C.) A method of financing retirement.

    D.) All of the above.

2.) What are two factors that should be considered when choosing a Periodic Withdrawal?

    A.) Inflation and investment volatility.

    B.) The rate of change in expenses and economic growth.

    C.) Deflation and economic stagnation.

    D.) A and C.

CHAPTER TWO

INVESTMENT VOLATILITY

Investment Volatility simply means that an investment's returns will fluctuate over time. Most everyone is aware of this in the abstract, but very few people are cognizant of the risk that this poses to their retirement income.

This chapter will explain how investment volatility is obscured by average returns. The incremental returns from the S&P 500 index will be used to assist in illustrating this.

Portia Prescott Teaches the Online Video Portion of the Training

S&P 500 AVERAGE ONE YEAR RETURNS

YEAR	RETURN	YEAR	RETURN	YEAR	RETURN
2012	16.00%	1991	30.47%	1970	4.01%
2011	2.11%	1990	-3.10%	1969	-8.50%
2010	15.06%	1989	31.69%	1968	11.06%
2009	26.46%	1988	16.61%	1967	23.98%
2008	-37.00%	1987	5.25%	1966	-10.06%
2007	5.49%	1986	18.67%	1965	12.45%
2006	15.79%	1985	31.73%	1964	16.48%
2005	4.91%	1984	6.27%	1963	22.80%
2004	10.88%	1983	22.56%	1962	-8.73%
2003	28.68%	1982	21.55%	1961	26.89%
2002	-22.10%	1981	-4.92%	1960	0.47%
2001	-11.89%	1980	32.50%	1959	11.96%
2000	-9.10%	1979	18.44%	1958	43.36%
1999	21.04%	1978	6.56%	1957	-10.78%
1998	28.58%	1977	-7.18%	1956	6.55%
1997	33.36%	1976	23.84%	1955	31.56%
1996	22.96%	1975	37.20%	1954	52.62%
1995	37.58%	1974	-26.47%	1953	-0.99%
1994	1.32%	1973	-14.66%	1952	18.37%
1993	10.08%	1972	18.98%	1951	24.02%
1992	7.62%	1971	14.31%	1950	31.71%

The average annual return for the entire 63-year period charted above is 11.03%. If you shared this average with someone that did not have access to the chart, and asked them to guess at the high and low return for the entire 63 years, they would have no basis upon which to provide an answer.

This is because the average is designed to indicate the central value of a dataset. To do so, it also completely obscures the volatility of the underlying data.

Because we have access to the chart, we can determine that the greatest return over the 63 years is a positive 52.62%, while the greatest loss is a negative 37.00%.

Unfortunately, in the financial industry average returns are the primary focus, and incremental returns are often ignored. Because of this, charts such as the previous one (which provide an easy methods of observing risk) are under-utilized.

Instead, a number of risk measures such as a **Standard Deviation**, Alpha, or R-squared are often used to describe risk. Although many individuals are comfortable with these statistics, they can be confusing to the layman.

Below is a table which has taken the incremental returns from the last table and placed them in the average return format that is commonly used in the financial industry.

S&P 500 AVERAGE ANNUAL TRAILING RETURNS
FOR THE PERIOD ENDING...

DATE	1 YEAR	3 YEAR	5 YEAR	10 YEAR	15 YEAR	20 YEAR
12/31/2012	16.0%	10.9%	1.7%	3.3%	4.5%	8.2%

Once again, the 20-year average return of 8.2% provides no indication that there was a 37% loss one year. And this information is exceedingly important for the retiree committed to drawing income to meet living expenses.

The reason that this is so important is that the great advantage of investing during the saving years begins to work against the individual in the withdrawal years.

This advantage is simply being able to invest in a down market when: **1)** buying low will maximize the number of shares purchased, and **2)** a long time-horizon will allow the shares to increase in value once the market recovers.

Just the opposite holds true in retirement. Selling shares at the bottom means having to sell more shares, and once that money has been spent, there is zero prospect of any further growth. Therefore, a 37% loss early in retirement might threaten the viability of the entire income stream.

The next chapter will provide a specific example of how volatility can disrupt a periodic withdrawal. But first, take a few moments to review the chart that follows, which contains the trailing return history for the S&P 500 for each calendar year going back to 1981.

S&P 500 ROLLING AVERAGE ANNUAL RETURNS

DATE	1 YEAR	3 YEAR	5 YEAR	10 YEAR	15 YEAR	20 YEAR
2012	*16.0%*	10.9%	1.7%	3.3%	4.5%	*8.2%*
2011	*2.1%*	14.1%	-0.2%	1.4%	5.5%	7.8%
2010	*15.1%*	-2.9%	2.3%	0.7%	6.8%	9.1%
2009	*26.5%*	-5.6%	0.4%	-0.5%	8.0%	8.2%
2008	*-37.0%*	-8.4%	-2.2%	-0.7%	6.5%	8.4%
2007	*5.5%*	8.6%	12.8%	2.8%	10.5%	11.8%
2006	*15.8%*	10.4%	6.2%	3.9%	10.6%	11.8%
2005	*4.9%*	14.4%	0.5%	4.2%	11.5%	11.9%
2004	*10.9%*	3.6%	-2.3%	5.6%	10.9%	13.2%
2003	*28.7%*	-4.1%	-0.6%	5.1%	12.2%	13.0%
2002	*-22.1%*	-14.6%	-0.6%	4.3%	11.5%	12.7%
2001	*-11.9%*	-1.0%	10.7%	6.0%	13.7%	15.2%
2000	*-9.1%*	12.3%	18.3%	8.0%	16.0%	15.7%
1999	*21.0%*	27.6%	28.6%	8.3%	18.9%	17.9%
1998	*28.6%*	28.2%	24.1%	8.7%	17.9%	17.8%
1997	*33.4%*	31.2%	20.3%	8.2%	17.5%	16.7%
1996	*23.0%*	19.7%	15.2%	7.0%	16.8%	14.6%
1995	*37.6%*	15.3%	16.6%	6.8%	14.8%	14.6%
1994	*1.3%*	6.3%	8.7%	6.6%	14.5%	14.6%
1993	*10.1%*	15.6%	14.5%	6.9%	15.7%	12.8%
1992	7.6%	10.8%	15.9%	7.4%	15.5%	11.3%
1991	30.5%	18.5%	15.4%	8.0%	14.3%	11.9%
1990	-3.1%	14.2%	13.2%	6.4%	13.9%	11.2%
1989	31.7%	17.4%	20.4%	8.0%	16.6%	11.6%
1988	16.6%	13.4%	15.3%	7.5%	12.2%	9.5%

S&P 500 ROLLING AVERAGE ANNUAL RETURNS
(CONTD)

1987	5.3%	18.1%	16.5%	7.0%	9.9%	9.3%
1986	18.7%	18.4%	19.9%	6.4%	10.8%	10.2%
1985	31.7%	19.7%	14.7%	6.6%	10.5%	8.7%
1984	6.3%	16.5%	14.8%	6.8%	8.8%	7.8%
1983	22.6%	12.3%	17.3%	4.9%	7.7%	8.3%
1982	21.6%	15.3%	14.1%	3.1%	7.0%	8.3%
1981	-4.9%	14.3%	8.1%	3.0%	7.1%	6.8%

In reviewing the chart, a comparison of a 20-year average annual return in the far right column with the incremental returns on the far left, will provide further evidence that average annual returns obscure volatility.

To see data going all the way back to 1950, be sure to visit the associated website at:

MyRetirementLibrary.com

CONCLUSION

If you're using a **Periodic Withdrawal** to cover your living expenses, **Investment Volatility** is a dangerous enemy that you cannot afford to ignore.

Incremental returns provide an easy method of gauging investment volatility, but unfortunately, this information is usually supplanted by average annual returns.

In order to plan properly for retirement, you have to be aware of **Investment Volatility** and incorporate it into your income model.

CHAPTER TWO QUESTIONS

T or **F**   1.) The S&P 500 represents the largest 500 publicly traded companies in the U.S.

T or **F**   2.) From year to year, a diversified pool of stocks can produce a wide range of returns.

T or **F**   3.) To understand the volatility of an investment, you need to view only the average annual returns that are published quarterly.

T or **F**   4.) A popular measurement of volatility is the Standard Deviation.

CHAPTER THREE

WHAT IS ASSET EROSION?

Investment Volatility can lead to **Asset Erosion,** and in its extreme, this means running out of money prematurely.

To illustrate how an unrealistic set of assumptions can lead to Asset Erosion, consider the one-year S&P 500 returns from 2002 to 2006. The average annual return over this five-year period is 6.2%. The individual one-year returns over this period are: -22.10%, 28.68%, 10.88%, 4.91% and 15.79%, respectively.

Doing a little financial math, George determined that at a rate of 6.2%, he can spread a balance of $300,000 over 5 years by withdrawing $67,426 per year. This scenario is shown on the following chart:

AVERAGE RETURN SCENARIO

YEAR	RETURN	BEG BAL	W/D	END BAL
2002	6.2%	300,000	67,426	246,994
2003	6.2%	246,994	67,426	190,701
2004	6.2%	190,701	67,426	130,918
2005	6.2%	130,918	67,426	67,426
2006	6.2%	67,426	67,426	0

Notably, there is no investment volatility, and therefore, no possibility of asset erosion. However, this is about to change.

In the second scenario, George's assumptions have not changed, but the average returns have been replaced with the actual incremental one-year returns that make up that 6.2% average:

ACTUAL RETURN SCENARIO

DATE	RETURN	BEG BAL	W/D	END BAL
2002	-22.10%	300,000	67,426	181,175
2003	28.68%	181,175	67,426	146,372
2004	10.88%	146,372	67,426	87,536
2005	4.91%	87,536	67,426	21,097
2006	15.79%	21,097	67,426	-53,644

As you can see, by the end of the fifth year the second scenario has developed a shortfall of -$53,644. The average return has obviously hidden some very important information from George: the volatility associated with the investment return.

14

Someone that plans for the average returns in the first scenario, but has to live with the actual returns in the second scenario is going to experience asset erosion. As can be seen in the second table, all it takes is one bad year early in the process to create an irreversible snowballing effect which dooms the entire enterprise.

CONCLUSION

In order to address **Investment Volatility** and the potential for **Asset Erosion**, you need to understand that volatility is not revealed by the average return, but by the incremental returns.

Another measurement of volatility is the **Standard Deviation**. In the following chapters, we'll lay out a foundation to begin to understand the standard deviation. Then, we can use this tool to add volatility to our model.

CHAPTER THREE QUESTIONS

1.) What causes Asset Erosion?

    A.) Assuming that your investment will earn a steady return, even though it exhibits volatility.

    B.) Withdrawing more than can be supported by your investment's earnings.

    C.) Having to draw from your investments while they are losing money.

    D.) All of the above.

2.) Why is it dangerous to use an average rate of return in your retirement assumptions?

    A.) An average return will hide volatility.

    B.) Fluctuations in returns over short periods will greatly impact the amount of money that can be generated to meet expenses.

    C.) Actually, you should use an average rate of return when planning for retirement.

    D.) A and B

3.) If you assume a flat rate of inflation in your assumptions…

A.) You may run out of money before you expected.

B.) You may have more money than you expected.

C.) Both A and B are true, but the greater concern is A.

CHAPTER FOUR

THE FREQUENCY CHART

In this chapter, we'll review the **Frequency Chart** and the **Bell Curve Distribution**. This will provide a foundation for discussing the **Standard Deviation**.

A frequency chart plots the results of a recurring event, such as the repeated flipping of a coin. If you flipped a coin 50 times and recorded the results, your frequency chart would have two columns: one for heads and one for tails. In a perfect world, each result would occur 25 times and your chart would look like this:

FREQUENCY CHART OF HEADS AND TAILS

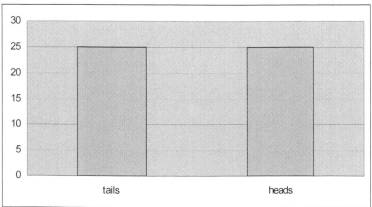

Rather than plotting the flip of a coin, however, let's chart investment returns. Instead of two possible outcomes, let's suppose that the following market returns occurred over a 26 year timeframe:

HYPOTHETICAL MARKET RETURNS

YEAR	RETURN	YEAR	RETURN
1	5%	14	0%
2	20%	15	-5%
3	-5%	16	5%
4	10%	17	5%
5	0%	18	5%
6	5%	19	15%
7	-10%	20	5%
8	5%	21	10%
9	-5%	22	5%
10	10%	23	0%
11	15%	24	5%
12	15%	25	5%
13	0%	26	10%

We can fit this data on a frequency chart, much in the same way we charted the coin flipping data.

On the next chart, the X-Axis shows the return; while the Y-Axis shows how many times that particular return occurred. For instance, the 5% return occurred 10 times.

EXAMPLE OF A FREQUENCY CHART

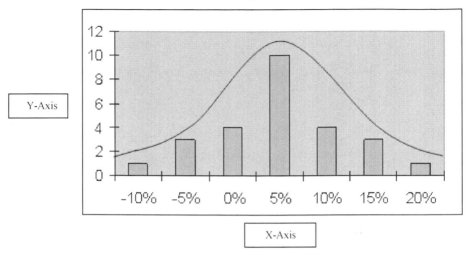

The set of values depicted on this chart is called a distribution and the shape of the distribution is symmetrical (the average is in the middle and each side of the distribution is a mirror-image of the other).

THE BELL CURVE DISTRIBUTION

A set of data, like the one above, can be described as a **Bell Curve Distribution**. As the name implies, the distribution of the data resembles the shape of a bell. Quite often, large sets of data take on this shape.

A bell curve distribution has an equal number of occurrences on either side of the average, with most occurrences falling close to the average.

CONCLUSION

Investment returns can be plotted on a **Frequency Chart** and very often the data will take on the shape of a bell curve.

A perfect **Bell Curve Distribution** has an equal number of observations on either side of the average, and most of these observation will occur close to the average.

A **Standard Deviation** is very effective in describing the volatility of this sort of distribution. We will discuss this measure next.

CHAPTER FOUR QUESTIONS

T or **F** 1.) A Frequency Chart allows you to see how often values occur within a specific range.

T or **F** 2.) A Bell Curve Distribution is the shape formed by many large sets of observations.

T or **F** 3.) A Bell Curve Distribution is humped in the middle and has tails on each side.

T or **F** 4.) A Bell Curve Distribution is often the shape depicted when plotting data on of a frequency chart.

CHAPTER FIVE

THE STANDARD DEVIATION

An **Average** is a statistical measure that helps to describe a dataset, and the same can be said about the **Standard Deviation**. While an average describes the central value of the dataset, a standard deviation helps to explain how many of the data-points are close to the average, and how many are further away from the average.

A standard deviation helps divide a dataset into three distinct groups. The first group includes values close to the average, the second includes values a medium distance from the average, and the third group includes values far away from the average. The next sections will lay this out in more detail.

THE FIRST STANDARD DEVIATION

If an investment has an average return of 8% and a Standard Deviation of 12 (and the distribution adheres to a standard bell curve), a randomly selected historical return should fall between

-4% and +20% about sixty-eight percent of the time. This is the upper and lower range of the **First Standard Deviation**.

The -4% is calculated by subtracting the standard deviation from the average (8% minus 12%), while the +20% is calculated by adding the standard deviation to the average (8% plus 12%).

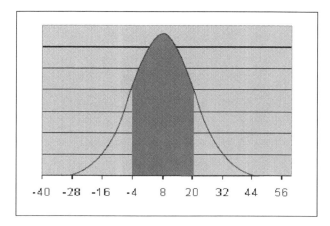

When the first standard deviation is shaded on a frequency chart, as above, there is still an undefined area under the curve that is not explained. Returns can also occur in this undefined area, most of which is contained within the second standard deviation.

THE SECOND STANDARD DEVIATION

The **Second Standard Deviation** explains how often data points should occur a medium distance from the average.

The second standard deviation begins where the first standard deviation ends (-4% and 20%).

Assuming an 8% return and a standard deviation of 12, expect returns within the second standard deviation to fall between -16% and -4% (on the left side of the bell curve) and between 20% and 32% (on the right side of the bell curve). Values should fall within these ranges about 27% percent of the time.

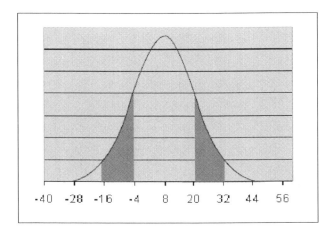

The high end of this range is calculated by adding a multiple of 2 times the standard deviation to the average:

$$8\% + (2 \times 12\%) = 32\%$$

And the low end of the range is calculated by subtracting 2 times the standard deviation from the average:

$$8\% - (2 \times 12\%) = -16\%$$

If the first and second standard deviations are combined, the probability of a value occurring between -16% and +32% is about

95.5% (this is the 68% probability of the first standard deviation added to the 27% of the second standard deviation).

THE THIRD STANDARD DEVIATION

This still leaves a tiny bit of area at either end of the bell curve. These two areas are where extreme values occur. Just over 2% of the time, values will occur beyond -16% (and up to -28%) on the lower end and beyond 32% (and up to 44%) on the higher end.

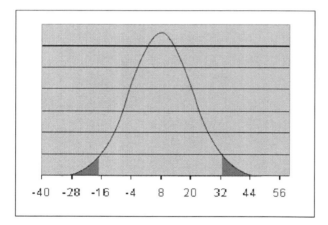

For the lower range of the **Third Standard Deviation,** the calculation would be:

$$8\% - (3 \times 12\%) = -28\%$$

For the upper range of the third standard deviation, the calculation would be:

$$8\% + (3 \times 12\%) = 44\%$$

By combining all three standard deviations, it can be stated that 99.7 percent of the time, values will occur between -28% and +44%. There is a slight chance of a return occurring beyond the third standard deviation.

CONCLUSION

The **Standard Deviation** is a way to measure the probability that an outcome will occur near the average, a medium distance from the average, or far away from the average.

In the next chapter, we'll use the standard deviation as a parameter for creating random returns, which will allow us to add **Investment Volatility** to the **Periodic Withdrawal**.

CHAPTER FIVE QUESTIONS

T or **F**   1.) If a distribution is shaped like a bell curve, about 68% of observations will fall within the first standard deviation.

T or **F**   2.) No observation can ever occur beyond the third standard deviation.

T or **F**   3.) A standard deviation is a way to measure how likely it is that an observation will fall a certain distance from the mean.

T or F   4.) If there is no volatility in a dataset, the standard deviation will equal zero.

CHAPTER SIX

ADDING VOLATILITY TO THE PERIODIC WITHDRAWAL MODEL

Chapter One introduced **Periodic Withdrawal** using a static 7.5% rate of return. This produced a steady and predictable income which would last indefinitely.

Unfortunately, that model wasn't realistic because it didn't include **Investment Volatility**. In this chapter, this oversight will be remedied by introducing a calculator that can generate random returns that are parameterized by an average return and a **Standard Deviation**.

A standard deviation of 18 alongside an average return of 7.5% will be used to mimic a stock investment. By doing so, the calculator will generate returns between -10.5% and 25.5% about 68 percent of the time, between -28.5% and 43.5%, about 27 percent of the time, and between -46.5% and 61.5% about 2 percent of the time.

(The decision to use a particular average and standard deviation is fraught with modeling risk. The statistics can be based on historical observations, however, there is no guarantee that future returns will follow historical patterns. Although this risk exists, there is a greater risk if volatility is ignored altogether.)

Following is the full set of assumptions:

ASSUMPTIONS

Starting Age: 65
Lifespan: 100
Beginning Balance: $860,000
Annual Withdrawal: $60,000
Average Return: 7.5%
Standard Deviation: 18

By entering these assumptions into the **Periodic Withdrawal Graphing Calculator** and clicking the **CALCULATE** button, a set of results will be produced which might look something like those below. In this instance, the income has grown handsomely:

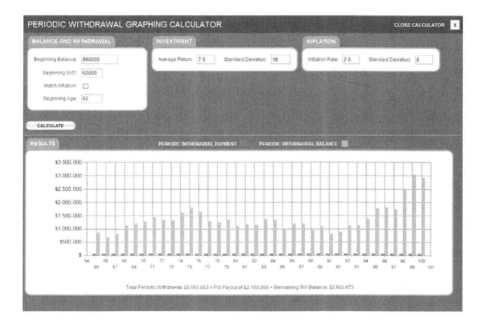

But this is only one possible outcome. Since the returns are generated randomly each time the **CALCULATE** button is clicked, any number of outcomes is possible. Below, a different set of results is shown, even though the set of assumptions did not change. In this case, negative returns were generated early in the withdrawal timeline, and asset erosion was the result:

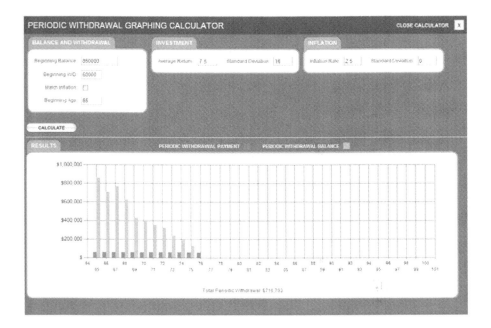

CONCLUSION

Although we've generated only two sets of results in this chapter, we can see that by adding random returns that are parameterized with a **Standard Deviation**, a wide range of outcomes are possible.

By running the calculator repeatedly, we can see a number of different outcomes. And Although this is helpful, the results are somewhat anecdotal.

The calculator is not set up to record the data, so we're currently limited to visually observing the results, or recording the results by hand. The first method is not very scientific, and the second is painstaking.

We'll remedy this by modifying the calculator to record the results and apply some statistical analysis.

But before we get that far, we should first introduce another important factor that George forgot to consider: **Inflation**.

CHAPTER SIX QUESTIONS

T or F 1.) One way to mimic stock returns is to use a random number generator that is parameterized for an average return and a standard deviation.

T or F 2.) Random returns will cause an income model to generate a different outcome each time the model is run, even if the inputs do not change.

T or F 3.) The average return is the only input needed to produce a realistic retirement income model.

CHAPTER SEVEN

INFLATION

Inflation is the other important factor that George left out of his retirement model.

Inflation, the phenomenon of rising prices, is an almost inevitable consequence of living in a modern economy. Every recorded civilization has produced evidence of inflation. With odds like that, it would behoove us to take the conservative approach and incorporate it into our retirement plans.

Just as with investment returns, future inflation cannot be predicted with accuracy. The best course of action is to study past behavior, incorporate likely possibilities into our model, and realize that future events may not look anything like what has transpired before.

Below is a chart showing average inflation rates for the 1, 3, 5, 10, 15 and 20-year periods using the Consumer Price Index (CPI) data available through the U.S. Bureau of Labor Statistics. Although this chart only goes back to 1992, you can see the data going back as far as 1913 by logging into the **My Retirement Library** website.

CPI AVERAGE INFLATION

Years	\multicolumn{6}{c}{AVERAGE ANNUAL INFLATION}
	1	3	5	10	15	20
2012	2.07%	2.29%	2.06%	2.47%	2.42%	2.49%
2011	3.16%	1.47%	2.22%	2.42%	2.43%	2.54%
2010	**1.64%**	1.69%	2.23%	**2.39%**	2.42%	2.59%
2009	**-0.36%**	2.09%	2.58%	2.56%	2.50%	2.78%
2008	**3.84%**	3.30%	3.19%	2.82%	2.69%	3.04%
2007	**2.85%**	3.15%	2.88%	2.59%	2.64%	3.05%
2006	**3.23%**	3.09%	2.63%	2.54%	2.65%	3.09%
2005	**3.39%**	2.78%	2.55%	2.51%	2.71%	3.03%
2004	**2.66%**	2.17%	2.54%	2.46%	2.85%	3.03%
2003	**2.28%**	2.23%	2.45%	2.45%	2.99%	3.12%
2002	**1.58%**	2.59%	2.31%	2.52%	3.11%	3.16%
2001	**2.85%**	2.80%	2.45%	2.66%	3.25%	3.39%
2000	3.36%	2.37%	2.47%	2.80%	3.18%	3.75%
1999	2.21%	2.02%	2.37%	3.00%	3.20%	4.24%
1998	1.56%	2.27%	2.44%	3.26%	3.34%	4.69%
1997	2.29%	2.69%	2.73%	3.52%	3.45%	4.99%
1996	2.95%	2.78%	2.87%	3.65%	3.71%	5.20%
1995	2.83%	2.80%	3.12%	3.54%	4.18%	5.34%
1994	2.56%	2.85%	3.63%	3.62%	4.87%	5.66%
1993	2.99%	3.40%	4.08%	3.79%	5.45%	6.08%
1992	3.01%	4.20%	4.31%	3.81%	5.76%	6.24%

To illustrate the danger of failing to incorporate inflation into a retirement plan, let's go back in time to the year 2001 and assume that George planned on spending $5,000 a year on groceries until the year 2010.

At the time, let's assume that he made a canny prediction that inflation would average 2.39% over that period. Doing a little financial math, he determined that he would need to put aside a total of $56,607 (to simplify the example, we'll assume that the $5,000 is spent on food at the beginning of the year, and that there is no investment return). This scenario is depicted in the table below:

AVERAGE (STATIC) INFLATION

YEAR	INFLATION	FOOD COST	BALANCE
			55,735
1	2.39%	5,000	50,735
2	2.39%	5,120	45,616
3	2.39%	5,242	40,374
4	2.39%	5,367	35,007
5	2.39%	5,495	29,511
6	2.39%	5,627	23,884
7	2.39%	5,761	18,123
8	2.39%	5,899	12,224
9	2.39%	6,040	6,184
10	2.39%	6,184	0

When subject to average inflation, the money lasted just long enough for George to buy groceries over the ten years. But what if George's assumptions were subjected to the actual inflation rates over that timeframe? The answer is below:

ACTUAL INFLATION

YEAR	INFLATION	FOOD COST	BALANCE
			55,735
1	2.85%	5,000	50,735
2	1.58%	5,142	45,593
3	2.28%	5,224	40,369
4	2.66%	5,343	35,027
5	3.39%	5,485	29,542
6	3.23%	5,671	23,871
7	2.85%	5,854	18,017
8	3.84%	6,020	11,997
9	-0.36%	6,252	5,745
10	1.64%	6,229	-484

As you can see, ignoring volatility has led to a $484 shortfall. This 7.8% shortfall means that George went without food for the last 28 days of the tenth year.

CONCLUSION

This chapter illustrates the risk of using a static inflation rate. In reality, inflation demonstrates volatility, just like investments do.

In the next chapter, we'll incorporate both static inflation and volatile inflation into the **Periodic Withdrawal Model**.

CHAPTER SEVEN QUESTIONS

1.) Why is it dangerous to use an average inflation rate in your retirement assumptions?

   A.) An average will hide volatility.

   B.) Fluctuations in inflation over short periods will greatly impact the amount of income that needs to be budgeted to cover expenses.

   C.) Actually, using an average rate of inflation is better than ignoring inflation altogether.

   D.) All of the above.

T or **F**   2.) To begin to understand inflation volatility, it is a good idea to review inflation rates over short periods of time.

T or **F**   3.) Ignoring the variable nature of inflation may cause you to experience Asset Erosion.

CHAPTER EIGHT

ADDING INFLATION TO THE PERIODIC WITHDRAWAL MODEL

The corrosive effects of inflation can be observed by adding a static rate of inflation of 2.5% to the baseline set of assumptions. The new set of assumptions look like this:

ASSUMPTIONS

Starting Age: 65
Lifespan: 100
Beginning Balance: $860,000
Annual Withdrawal: $60,000
Average Return: 7.5%
Average Inflation: 2.5%

When the calculator displays the results, it will be apparent that the payments are increasing each year (the blue/darker bars). This is because they're rising with inflation to allow George to maintain the same purchasing power year after year.

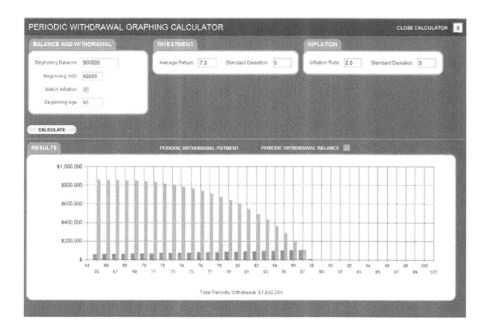

Also note that using this set of assumptions causes the periodic withdrawal to run dry by age 87. This is a startling outcome. In the original scenario (without inflation) the income lasted indefinitely.

But things could get worse. Next, volatility will be added to both the investment return and inflation rate to determine their combined effect on the model.

ADDING INVESTMENT AND INFLATION VOLATILITY

This example includes a standard deviation of 18 for the investment return, and 2.5 for inflation. This will create a different set of results each time that the calculator is run, so multiple sets of results will be shown below.

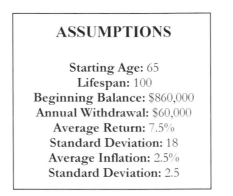

ASSUMPTIONS

Starting Age: 65
Lifespan: 100
Beginning Balance: $860,000
Annual Withdrawal: $60,000
Average Return: 7.5%
Standard Deviation: 18
Average Inflation: 2.5%
Standard Deviation: 2.5

The screenshot below shows the first set of results. Notice that the introduction of volatility has caused the income stream to terminate at age 77 (versus age 87 in the previous example).

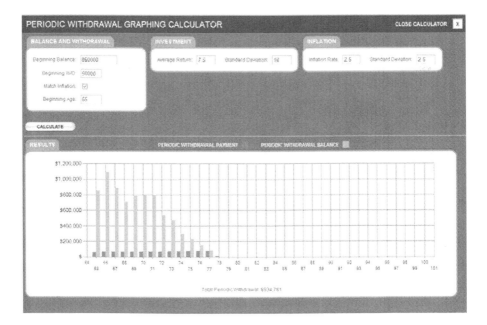

If run several more times, eventually get a more favorable result will occur. Below is one such possible outcome.

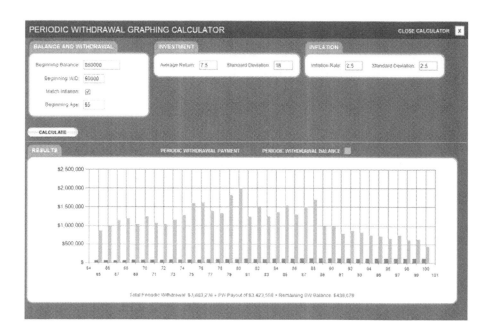

In this case, a strong bull market was realized and the balance grew to a mind-boggling sum before receding. Actually, this particular result is not very realistic.

This outcome is the effect of the parameters in place. Since only an average and standard deviation were used in the **Random Number Generator**, there was nothing to stop a very long series of strong returns from occurring. In a more sophisticated model, a method may be employed to avoid unlikely outcomes such as this by causing a reversion to the average.

Although out of the ordinary, once a large enough dataset of results is gathered and analyzed, the effects of these extreme outcomes will be minimized, so that some reasonable conclusions can be drawn about the retirement assumptions.

To accomplish this, the calculator will be modified to run through a thousand scenarios at a time, record the output, and perform statistical analysis. But first, the next section of the book will introduce some variations of the periodic withdrawal model, as well as introduce the variable life annuity.

CONCLUSION

Adding **Inflation Volatility** to the **Periodic Withdrawal** model may cause the income stream to terminate much earlier than anticipated.

In order to minimize this risk, you should consider drawing a smaller income, investing in less risky assets, utilizing an **Asset Cost Averaging** strategy, or selecting an annuity income for a part or all of your retirement income needs. These strategies are introduced in the next chapter.

CHAPTER EIGHT QUESTIONS

1.) If you add inflation to a withdrawal model, the income stream will:

   A.) Last just as long as a similar model in which inflation was absent.

   B.) Last for a longer period of time than a similar model in which inflation was absent.

   C.) Last for a shorter period of time than a similar model in which inflation was absent.

   D.) None of the above.

T or F   2.) A model that includes both inflation volatility and investment volatility will be more unpredictable than a model in which only investment volatility is present.

3.) Ways to minimize the risk of a periodic withdrawal include:

   A.) Drawing a smaller amount.

   B.) Investing in less risky assets.

   C.) A and B.

   D.) None of the above.

PART II

CHAPTER NINE

STRATEGIES TO MAKE A PERIODIC WITHDRAWAL LAST?

Based on the analysis so far, you can see that implementing a **Periodic Withdrawal** can be a very risky strategy. Success depends on either having a very large amount of money in proportion to the desired income stream, or being lucky enough to experience strong growth in your investments, particularly in the early years of retirement. You may want to consider increasing your chances for success by applying one or more of the following strategies briefly explained below:

FUNNEL METHOD

Instead of drawing your funds directly from the risky asset, you can create a funnel. In this scenario, over time your invested dollars move from riskier investments to less risky investments and finally to safe investments. This creates a buffer that should help reduce the effects of **Asset Erosion**.

This is akin to matching a risk level with your time horizon. You would withdraw from the low risk assets while money earmarked for withdrawal in the distant future would remain invested in risky assets.

ASSET COST AVERAGING

Asset Cost Averaging concentrates on withdrawing income based on a number of shares rather than based on a dollar amount. In the following example the number of shares remains constant, but the amount of the withdrawal fluctuates. This is just the opposite of what most people actually do, which is to draw a stable dollar amount, and allow the number of shares that have to be sold to fluctuate.

This option is not all that popular because most individuals need to budget for a fixed set of expenses, which is difficult to do when your income is constantly fluctuating.

ASSET COST AVERAGING

Period	Shares	Share Price	Income
1	200	11.21	2,242
2	200	10.69	2,138
3	200	10.99	2,198
4	200	10.56	2,112
5	200	10.08	2,016
6	200	9.37	1,874
7	200	9.67	1,934
8	200	10	2,000
9	200	9.93	1,986
10	200	10.12	2,024

DIVERSIFIED ASSET ALLOCATION

A **Diversified Asset Allocation** simply means that you own a mixture of investments, i.e., stocks, bonds, mutual funds, money market instruments, etc. These investments are expected to perform differently over time, helping to shield from the possibility of asset erosion. You may draw from one, or a little from each, depending on the mix of performance.

ORDERLY WITHDRAWAL METHOD

The **Orderly Withdrawal Method** suits those with assets invested across a range of investment choices and products, much like the diversified asset allocation method. However, with this method you would take into account levels of risk, taxation, and regulation, in order to set priorities and withdraw funds in a manner that is the most advantageous.

CONCLUSION

This has been a very brief introduction to additional withdrawal methods. It's purpose is to show that there are retirement income choices other than the basic **Periodic Withdrawal** featured in this volume. These additional methods may enhance the ability of your retirement to survive.

An additional income option that may reduce the risk of **Asset Erosion** is called the **Variable Life Annuity**. We'll introduce this product in the next chapter and focus on it for the remainder of the book.

CHAPTER NINE QUESTIONS

1.) Stretching the life of a periodic withdrawal can include strategies such as:

A.) The Funnel Method.

B.) Asset Cost Averaging.

C.) The Random Withdrawal Method.

D.) A and B.

CHAPTER TEN

TYPES OF ANNUITIES

One of the most common products used to generate retirement income is called an **Annuity**. Unfortunately, the term "Annuity" can mean many different things. In its simplest form, an annuity is an income stream.

A typical annuity agreement would go something like this: George gives XYZ Insurance Company $500,000 today, and XYZ Insurance Company agrees to pay George $2,500 a month for as long as he lives.

More broadly, the term "Annuity" may refer to a product that has the option of being converted to an annuity income, even if that feature is not mandatory and is never even chosen by the retiree.

A retirement savings account with an annuity option is often referred to as being either in the **Pay-in Phase** or in the **Pay-out Phase**. The pay-in phase represents the period over which contributions are made (it can be one large premium made right before retirement, or it can be a number of premiums made over a number of years leading up to retirement). The pay-out phase refers to the point after which the balance is converted to an annuity income.

The remainder of this chapter defines various kinds of annuities available in the marketplace, although it is not an exhaustive list.

ANNUITY CERTAIN

An **Annuity Certain** allows for an income stream that lasts for a fixed number of years. This is as opposed to a life annuity, which is paid out over the lifetime of a specific individual. Often the annuity company allows a fixed period to be chosen in 5 year increments, i.e., 5, 10, 15, or 20 years.

TRADITIONAL OR FIXED LIFE ANNUITY

A **Fixed Life Annuity** is a product that will provide a fixed income stream that will last for the life of the owner (also called the annuitant). The balance participates in the insurance company's general account, which usually holds bonds, real estate, loans, and other relatively stable investments. Once converted to a lifetime income, the payments will not fluctuate.

A variation on this product is called a **Traditional Annuity**. With this product, the payment will rise and fall with long term interest rates.

A fixed life annuity can also cover the life expectancy of two people. In this case, the income would continue for as long as one of the two annuitants is alive.

VARIABLE LIFE ANNUITY

A **Variable Life Annuity** allows the owner to select from among a number of different investment strategies. Investment choices my include asset classes such as stocks, bonds, money market instruments, real estate, etc., and may focus on a particular sector, industry, country, or region. Income, although variable, will last for the lifetime of the annuitant.

IMMEDIATE ANNUITY/ SINGLE PREMIUM ANNUITY (SPRIA)

A **SPRIA** is an annuity product that allows for a large one-time premium to be paid, after which, the income immediately begins.

TAX-DEFERRED ANNUITY

The chief feature of a **Tax-Deferred Annuity** is that contributions will reduce income for tax purposes. Also, any earnings on the funds accrue tax-free. However, upon withdrawal or annuitization normal income tax rates apply.

AFTER-TAX ANNUITY

An **After-Tax Annuity** is funded with after-tax dollars. In other words, contributions cannot be deducted for tax purposes. The good news is that earnings are tax-deferred. Upon withdrawal or annuitization, the portion of each withdrawal that represents earnings is taxed, while the portion that represents the contributions is returned tax-free.

PERSONAL ANNUITY

Generally, this term refers to an after-tax annuity. It is called a **Personal Annuity** because it is not sponsored by an employer. Contributions are made on an after tax basis. Earnings are deferred, and upon withdrawal or annuitization, the income is partially taxable based on the proportion of earnings and contributions.

FLEXIBLE PREMIUM ANNUITY

During the pay-in phase, a contract with a flexible premium provision will allow the owner to control the amount and frequency of the contributions.

EQUITY-INDEXED ANNUITY

The main feature of an **Equity-Indexed Annuity** involves how investment returns are credited. A floor and cap are used to adjust investment returns based on the performance of the underlying index. For instance, a product may allow investment in a stock mutual fund with a guarantee of a minimum return of 6% per year, but with a cap of 15%.

In this example, the policyholder/annuitant will not suffer losses in a down market (assuming that the company has strong financial backing and can pay during times of economic upheaval), but will give up any returns in excess of 15%. While one company may use the formula listed above, another may use a completely different formula, such as a 4% minimum with a 10% cap. There is no standardization for these kinds of annuities, so it is very important to read the contract language and understand it fully.

An **Equity-Indexed Annuity** appeals to the consumer that wants all gain and no loss. Because risk and return are two sides to the same coin, (i.e., higher returns mean undertaking greater risk) both desires cannot be fulfilled simultaneously.

While the consumer may believe that they are transferring market risk from themselves to the company, there are usually a number of fees, expenses, and contractual caveats, which allow the insurance company to reduce the amount of the payouts (and therefore the amount of risk the company undertakes, i.e. giving a smaller return back to the customer to match the reduced risk they are undertaking).

RETIREMENT ANNUITY

A **Retirement Annuity** is specifically designed for saving money for retirement and is often sponsored by an employer. Before retirement, the employer or employee may make contributions (before tax) into a number of different investment choices. Upon retirement, this product can be converted into a lifetime income or removed as cash. These kinds of plans usually operate under the 401(k) or 403(b) section of the tax code.

CONCLUSION

This chapter briefly defines types of annuity products. Each company may offer many unique features to their annuities that should be fully researched before any purchase is made.

CHAPTER TEN QUESTIONS

T or F 1.) One annuity is pretty much like any other annuity.

CHAPTER ELEVEN

ARE PENSIONS ALSO ANNUITIES?

PENSIONS

Pensions have annuity-like features and sometimes the word "pension" and "annuity" are used interchangeably. However, there is a difference between the two in regards to basic features and financing.

A pension is generally referred to as a **Defined-Benefit Plan**. Such a plan guarantees the employee a stream of income. The amount of income awarded is based on a formula that takes into account years of service, salary, and age. The payments generally begin at retirement and are paid for the life of the pensioner.

In a pension plan, the employer takes on the risk to fund the plan and make investment decisions.

If the employer makes poor decisions and finances fall short of requirements, they're still responsible for paying the benefits. Because of the high cost and risk that pensions represent to employers, they've fallen out of favor in private enterprise, but are still in use at all levels of government.

ANNUITIES

Annuities are often offered as a feature of a **Defined-Contribution Plan** such as a 401(k) or 403(b). In these plans, the dollar amount available at retirement is primarily dependent on the employee's ability to make contributions, and also to make good investment decisions. At retirement, the employee can exercise the annuity option (if available), make a complete withdrawal, or withdraw cash on a schedule.

CONCLUSION

Pensions and **Annuities** both share the goals of providing a retirement income, however, a pension transfers most of the associated risk to the employer, while an annuity is usually part of a retirement plan that transfers most of the risk to the employee.

CHAPTER ELEVEN QUESTIONS

1.) What are the main differences between a pension and an annuity?

    A.) A pension is primarily funded by an employer.

    B.) A pension is primarily funded by an employee.

    C.) A pension allows the employee to make investment decisions.

    D.) A pension usually allows for a lump sum withdrawal.

2.) The following is true about an annuity:

    A.) An annuity can be a feature provided within a 401(k) retirement plan.

    B.) A pension may behave like an annuity in that it may provide an income for the life of the pensioner.

    C.) A pension is usually not a true annuity.

    D.) All of the above.

CHAPTER TWELVE

ADVANTAGES OF ANNUITIES

The purpose of an annuity is to provide financial security in the form of a stream of income that cannot be outlived. Insurance companies accomplish this task, in part, by pooling risks.

POOLING OF RISKS

If many people are exposed to a particular risk, but only a few will actually succumb to it, the costs can be spread among the many, while the benefits can be concentrated among the few.

Home and auto insurance are examples of this. If you incur damage to your house or car, your insurance company will reimburse you for the loss. To qualify for this indemnification, you have to pay the premiums (but these premiums will amount to much less than the cost of a catastrophic event). The insurance company can afford to reimburse you for your loss because they have a multitude of other premium-paying clients (only a small portion of which will incur a loss).

This concept also applies to life annuities. "But Wait", you're thinking "no one can avoid death." That's true. But the risk being transferred to the insurance company is not whether death *will* occur, but rather *when* death will occur.

Although no one can know for certain when they'll die, it's statistically possible to determine the average life expectancy (and its associated standard deviation) for a large number of people. An insurance company can use this information to plan for the transfer of income from those that die early to those that live longer.

WHAT IS THE UPSIDE?

The upside is that if you live longer than the average life expectancy, you'll continue receiving income. Someone that began income in their mid-60s and lived to age 105 could receive about twice what they put into the contract.

PROTECTION FROM ASSET EROSION

A **Variable Annuity** is structured to protect you from asset erosion.

As mentioned in an earlier chapter, **Asset Erosion** can affect a **Periodic Withdrawal** if you earn less on your investments than you expected. If this occurs, you'll have to sell more shares to withdraw the amount of money you've budgeted to spend. This damages the prospects for future returns.

A variable annuity protects against this possibility by awarding a number of shares that do not have to be sold or exchanged to produce income. The number of 'annuity shares' owned remains static, and the amount of income received depends on the value of each share (which will rise and fall with the underlying investment).

Therefore, your income will drop if your investment loses value. However, unlike a periodic withdrawal, which may not recover from a downswing, the annuity income will "bounce back" when the stock market recovers.

However, the risk of completely running out of money is greatly diminished, and would require that the underlying investment permanently lose all value (not likely with a broadly diversified investment) or that the insurance company go out of business (be sure to research and pick a company with high ratings).

CONCLUSION

Insurance companies (that are financially sound) are in a much better position to manage a lifetime income and avoid asset erosion than most individuals. This is because an insurance company can pool risks.

CHAPTER TWELVE QUESTIONS

1.) Advantages of Annuities include:

A.) An income stream that will last a lifetime.

B.) The financial strength that comes from pooling risks.

C.) A and B.

D.) Complete control to do as you please with your retirement nest egg.

2.) Risks that an annuity may help you overcome include:

A.) The risk of living for an unusually long period of time and running out of income.

B.) The risk of asset erosion.

C.) All of the above.

CHAPTER THIRTEEN

DISADVANTAGES OF ANNUITIES

FINANCIAL RISK ASSOCIATED WITH THE INSURANCE COMPANY

Purchasing an annuity does have financial risks. First and foremost, the insurance company may not remain solvent, i.e., it could go bankrupt. The best way to protect yourself from this possibility is to research life insurance companies and deal only with those with the best financial records.

There are ratings agencies which review the financial statements of insurance companies and publish their findings. The four major ratings agencies are Duff and Phelps, AM Best, Standard and Poor's, and Fitch.

AN IRREVERSIBLE DECISION

The second important thing to consider is that an annuity usually can not be reversed. In other words, once you have converted your balance into an income stream, it can't be turned back into a lump sum. There may be some products available that will allow for this, but such a feature will cost more.

PREMATURE DEATH

Third, you need to consider the possibility that you may die prematurely. If this occurs, you may forfeit the income that you would have otherwise been paid (from the time of your death up until the average life expectancy that is in use).

In order to minimize the risk of premature death, some annuity products offer death benefits which guarantee that a minimum amount of income will continue to a survivor. One such option guarantees that income will continue for the first 20 years of the contract, whether the annuitant remains alive or not. That's pretty good protection for someone with a life expectancy of around 20 years, i.e., someone in their mid-sixties.

COSTS

Annuities often receive bad press because there are some very expensive products out there that have besmirched the rest of the industry. As you're shopping for an annuity, you should consider the many ways that an insurance company can charge you for their services. This includes things like back-end loads, front-end loads, commissions, management fees, record keeping fees, operating costs, and mortality expenses, etc. The next chapter will provide some definitions for the most common fees and expenses.

CONCLUSION

The potential drawbacks of an annuity include the financial risk of the insurance company, the inability to reverse the contract, the possibility of premature death, and costs. These are things which should be researched before making a final decision.

CHAPTER THIRTEEN QUESTIONS

1.) Four main things to investigate when reviewing any annuity product include:

   A.) The financial Strength of the insurance company.

   B.) The survivor benefits available to your loved ones if you die prematurely.

   C.) Whether the conversion to the annuity can be undone, and if so, at what cost.

   D.) Costs.

   E.) All of the above.

2.) Disadvantages of annuities include:

   A.) Income may stop at death if no additional protection is purchased. So if you die early, you'll have not received the full value of your investment.

   B.) Asset erosion may cause you to lose all of your income.

   C.) Since you cannot know for certain when you'll die, you will never receive the full value of your investment.

   D.) Shares are sold to provide the income stream.

CHAPTER FOURTEEN

ANNUITY EXPENSES

This chapter details some of the expenses that are associated with annuities. An affordable annuity product will charge only operating costs and mortality expenses. An expensive annuity product will charge additional fees, loads or commissions.

FRONT-END LOADS

A **Front-End Load** is a charge levied at the time the annuity is purchased. Annuities aren't the only products that may charge a front-end load. Mutual funds can also have them. The concept behind a front-end load is that a percentage of the initial investment is taken by the insurance company as a charge. Often this amount is paid directly to the agent. For instance, if the front-end load is 5% and the investment amount is $500,000, the amount of the load is $50,000. The amount actually invested is $450,000.

BACK-END LOADS

Back-End Loads, or surrender charges, are paid upon the withdrawal of funds from an annuity product that is in the pay-in phase. back-end loads are not a concern if an individual is planning to keep their annuity. These loads are often the highest in the first few years of a contract, but they may taper off, giving you the opportunity to withdraw your money penalty free.

For instance, in the first year, a load may be high, i.e., 7%. In the second and third year, it may drop to 6%, and in the next three years after that, the load might drop to 5%, 4%, and then 3%. Under this scenario, an individual who withdrew $6,000 at the end of the third year would have to pay the insurance company $360.

There are annuity products available that do not have front or back-end loads, so a bit of research is in order.

COMMISSIONS

A **Commission** on an annuity is just like a commission on any other type of product. It's a form of payment to the agent, and generally increases the price of the product.

MANAGEMENT FEES, OPERATING EXPENSES, ADVISORY FEES

Also called M&E fees, these are charges associated with the underlying investment choice. These are often broken down into an advisory fee and an operating expense. They need to be taken into consideration with all other fees that are charged to determine the overall cost of the product. **Management Fees** are deducted as operating costs from the investment portfolio.

RECORD KEEPING FEES

Record Keeping Fees, or administrative charges, are what the company is going to charge you for keeping track of your investment and sending required mailings. Not every company charges this fee.

CONTRACT MAINTENANCE FEE

A **Contract Maintenance Fee** represents the costs of maintaining the contract that an insurance company passes on to their clients.

MORTALITY EXPENSES

This is a charge that the annuity company uses to increase or decrease your payment based on the actual number of clients that have passed away. During a year, if more clients pass away, the **Mortality Expenses** will drop and you'll receive more money. On the other hand, if fewer die than expected, the expenses increase and your payments decrease.

CONCLUSION

There is a wide range of costs, fees, and expenses that insurance companies may wish to charge you. You should shop around and find an inexpensive product from a reputable company with high ratings.

CHAPTER FOURTEEN QUESTIONS

1.) Which costs associated with an annuity represent a commission?

A.) Front-end load.

B.) Back-end load.

C.) A and B.

2.) Which expense might turn into a credit in favor of the annuitant in a given year?

A.) Mortality expenses.

B.) Fees and expenses.

C.) Contract maintenance fee.

D.) All of the above.

CHAPTER FIFTEEN

LIFE ANNUITY INCOME OPTIONS

Just like other kinds of insurance, life annuities can offer different coverages—the greater the coverage the greater the cost.

SINGLE LIFE ANNUITY

The largest payment will be generated by a single life annuity. A **Single Life Annuity** covers just one person for their lifetime. At the end of their life, the payments stop.

JOINT AND SURVIVOR ANNUITY

Under this option, two individuals are covered. The income will continue until the last persons dies. There are variations on this in which the amount paid-out changes depending on which partner dies first.

For instance, you could have a **2/3 Benefit to Survivor** option in which the payment is reduced by 1/3 upon the death of one of the partners. Also, there could be a feature called **1/2 Benefit to Second Annuitant**. In this case, if the primary annuitant dies first, the payment is reduced by half, but if the secondary annuitant dies first, the payment isn't reduced. This may fit specific income replacement needs depending on what other sources of income may exist.

RESIDUAL DEATH BENEFITS

Secondary to providing a lifetime income, some annuity products are designed to allow for some financial protection to your heirs should you die prematurely. Survivor benefits are usually offered as a continuation of the income stream, but will only last for a set number of years. The clock starts ticking, not upon your death, but from when you initiated the income. This feature is sometimes referred to as a guaranteed period.

As an example, imagine that you purchase a single life annuity with a 15-year guaranteed period. If you die ten years into the contract, payments are due to your heirs for another five years. Or, your heirs have the option to take the benefit as a lump sum (which would result in receiving the present value of the future income stream).

CONCLUSION

Annuities can provide single life coverage, joint life coverage, and survivor benefits. To determine the specific options available, you should get quotes from many companies.

CHAPTER FIFTEEN QUESTIONS

1.) The term residual death benefit means:

A.) The annuity's primary purpose is to provide death benefits.

B.) The annuity's primary purpose is to avoid paying death benefits.

C.) The annuity's ancillary purpose is to provide death benefits.

2.) A single life annuity will:

A.) Stop paying income at death.

B.) May also provide a death benefit.

C.) Will continue paying to a second annuitant.

CHAPTER SIXTEEN

WHAT IS THE COST OF A LIFE ANNUITY?

It can be hard to determine the actual cost of a life annuity because the payments are based on actuarial considerations (that can be obscured by the insurance company for competitive reasons). One way to get a glimpse of the cost of a life annuity is to get a quote from a company for both a life annuity and a fixed period annuity. A fixed period annuity is similar to a life annuity product, but with a more straight forward premise. The main difference between the two, is that the fixed period annuity will last for a finite number of years, while the life annuity will last for the life of the annuitant (but with the payment calculation based on the average life expectancy of the entire pool of annuitants).

Therefore, if we could set the length of a fixed period annuity equal to the average life expectancy used in the life annuity calculation (with all other factors remaining equal), the difference in the payments would represent the cost of the insurance component needed to ensure payments beyond the average life expectancy. This would be the added cost of the life coverage.

ANNUITY LONGEVITY: LIFE VERSUS FIXED PERIOD

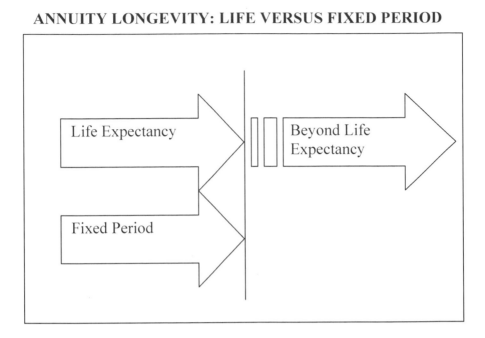

The method of comparison can be demonstrated by first obtaining a quote from an insurance company for a 20 year fixed period annuity, and also for a single life annuity for a 65 year old.

ASSUMPTIONS

Starting Age: 65
Beginning Balance: $860,000
AIR: 4%

The quote received was a payment of $4830 per month ($57,960 annually) for the fixed period annuity and $5,069 monthly ($60,828 annually) for the single life annuity.

The fact that the fixed period annuity payment is $239 less than the life annuity payment points to the fact that the life expectancy in use must be less than 20 years (the fewer the periods, the larger the payment). In this case, the insurance representative confirmed that the life expectancy is close to 17 years.

To create an equal comparison: adjust the number of periods in the fixed period annuity to equal 17, rather than 20. To do this, **1)** determine the growth rate used for the fixed period annuity, **2)** calculate a new payment based on the reduction in the number of periods and this rate, **3)** and finally, compare this new payment to the life annuity.

Step One: can be completed by using the RATE formula in Microsoft Excel to solve for the growth rate. Simply select any cell, and enter the following formula:

=RATE(20,57960,-894400,0,1)

This will return a rate of 2.9157%. The data in this formula includes: the number of years (20), the payment (57,960), the present value ($860,000, but inflated 4% for the AIR), the future value (0), and the 1 at the end denotes that the payments are made at the beginning of the year.

Step Two: now solve for the new payment. This can be done with the Microsoft Excel PMT formula:

=PMT(0.029157,17,-894400,0,1)

The result is that by shaving three years off the term, the payment from the fixed period annuity rises from $57,960 to $65,560 (The numbers in the formula are: the rate, number of periods, beginning balance, future value, and the 1 to indicate that that payments are made at the beginning of the period).

Step Three: Now that the term of the fixed period is equal to the life expectancy, compare the two payments. The life annuity will provide $60,828 annually, while the fixed period will provide $65,560, for a difference of $4,732 per year! That might sound like a huge amount, however, performing a break even analysis is important in determining how much longer the annuitant would have to live beyond the first 17 years in order to recoup the annual shortage of $4,732.

To do this determine the present value of the $4,732 shortfall each year for the first 17 years (discounted by the rate of 2.92%), and then determine how many annual payments of $60,828 (also discounted) must be made after the first 17 years before the loss is recouped.

PERIOD	FUTURE CASHFLOW	PRESENT VALUE OF CASHFLOWS DISCOUNTED AT 2.92%
1	($4,732)	($4,732)
2	($4,732)	($4,597)
3	($4,732)	($4,467)
4	($4,732)	($4,341)
5	($4,732)	($4,218)
6	($4,732)	($4,098)
7	($4,732)	($3,982)
8	($4,732)	($3,869)
9	($4,732)	($3,759)
10	($4,732)	($3,653)
11	($4,732)	($3,549)
12	($4,732)	($3,449)
13	($4,732)	($3,351)
14	($4,732)	($3,256)
15	($4,732)	($3,164)
16	($4,732)	($3,074)
17	($4,732)	($2,987)
18	$60,828	$37,318
19	$37,753	$22,505

As shown on the chart above, there are 17 periods of discounted cash flows for the amount of $4,732, which represents a total loss of $59,823 versus the fixed period annuity. Of course, after that 17 year period, the fixed period annuity would stop paying out, but the life annuity would continue (should the annuitant live beyond that time).

The life annuity would only have to continue paying out for 19 and a half months (all of year 18, and 7 ½ months of year 19) to achieve a present value of $59,823.

Of course, should the annuitant continue to live beyond that period, the payment would continue, so one way to think about this insurance component is to imagine, that the annual shortfall represents a premium paid to begin an income in 18 years that will continue for life.

VARIABLE INCOME ANNUITY

For the purposes of simplicity, the previous example does not consider adjustments to the annual income based on the investment experience of the underlying investment, and the Assumed Interest Rate (AIR).

MORTALITY EXPENSES

In addition to the normal operating expenses that any investment fund will experience, a life annuity will also have mortality expenses. Generally, mortality expenses and the lag factor will detract from the amount of the payment. However, depending on the adjustment that needs to be made in any given year, mortality expenses could be adjusted in favor of the annuitant. These expenses may cause an increase or decrease in the payments.

CONCLUSION

A **Fixed Period Annuity** can be used as an approximation of what a **Life Annuity** might pay, when comparing equal payment periods. This is only an approximation, but helps in determining the cost of a life annuity.

As well, the income provided by a **Variable Life Annuity** will fluctuate based on investment experience, the AIR, and expenses.

CHAPTER SIXTEEN QUESTIONS

1.) A life annuity is similar to a fixed annuity except:

   A.) Income continues as long as the annuitant is alive.

   B.) The additional cost of mortality expenses are included.

   C.) All of the above.

2.) The Assumed Interest rate is:

   A.) The growth rate used to determine the annuity payment.

   B.) A bonus percentage by which the company may credit the beginning balance.

   C.) The amount by which future investment returns are reduced.

   D.) All of the above.

   E.) None of the above.

PART III

CHAPTER SEVENTEEN

ADDING VOLATILITY TO A VARIABLE LIFE ANNUITY MODEL

In this Chapter, the **Variable Life Annuity** will be compared side by side with the **Periodic Withdrawal**.

Both income options will be subject to the same set of random returns in order to observe how each reacts under the same set of conditions.

As mentioned previously, the calculator creates volatility via a random number generator that uses an average, a standard deviation, and a bell curve distribution as parameters. As an example, if an average return of 10% and a standard deviation of 10 were used, 97% of the time, returns would fall between negative 10% and positive 30%.

In the screenshots that follow, the periodic withdrawal is represented by blue/dark bars, while the variable life annuity is represented by green/light bars. Since a different outcome is possible each time the calculator is run, there are multiple sets of results provided in this chapter for review. Below is the first:

ASSUMPTIONS
Starting Age: 65
Life Span: 100
Beginning Balance: $860,000
Annual Withdrawal: $60,000
Average Return: 7.5%
Standard Deviation: 18

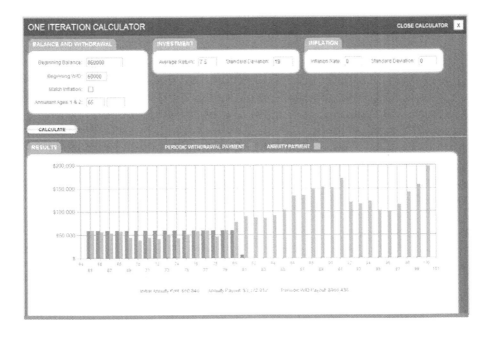

In this screenshot, the periodic withdrawal only lasts to age 80. This is because a series of negative returns led to asset erosion. While the periodic withdrawal paid out around $750 thousand dollars, the annuity paid out over $2.5 million.

Although there was a lot of growth in the annuity payment in the later years, the payment did shrink between the ages of 66 and 80. This decrease in income could adversely impact a retirement budget (unless the retiree has built a cushion, could borrow, or turn to other assets), and is considered the annuity version of asset erosion (although not as devastating). This phenomenon is referred to as the **Annuity Income Shortfall.** This concept, and how to deal with it, is described in more detail at the conclusion of this volume.

Below is another possible outcome for the same set of assumptions:

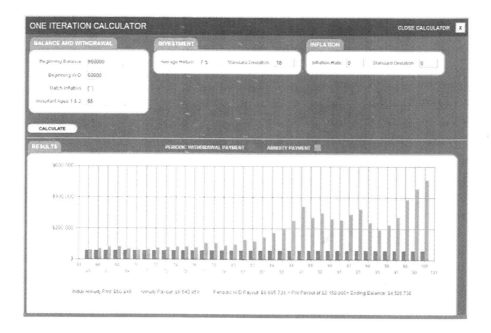

In this instance, the periodic withdrawal and the variable life annuity both lasted to age 100 and paid out amounts in the high $6 millions due to a very long bull market.

As mentioned in a previous chapter, strong results such as this one are the result of the set of parameters employed by the random number generator. Basically, there is no mechanism to cause a reversion to the mean in the event of a series of strong returns such as this. The impact of extreme outcomes like this one will be diminished once a large number of iterations are run and analyzed. In professional software, a method of reversion may exist, and you should ask your **Financial Planner** about the functionality and philosophy behind the parameters that are in use.

Below is a screenshot of the third result:

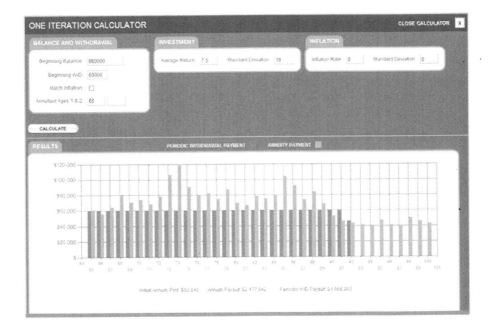

In this last scenario, the periodic withdrawal has lasted to age 92 and paid out $1.67 million, while the variable life annuity has lasted to age 100 and paid out $2.47 million.

Keep in mind that at age 90, the annuity payment fell below the initial payment amount of $60,000. This may not be a problem if the retiree saved money in the early years when income exceeded the budget. However, if this didn't happen, the annuitant could be facing a budget crunch and would have to turn to other assets, or borrow, in order to meet his or her budget.

This is another example of an **Annuity Income Shortfall**, which is addressed in more detail at the end of the volume.

ADDITIONAL POINTS

This section describes the model in the calculator in greater detail:

Hypothetical versus Actual Annuity Pricing - *The annuity payments presented here are hypothetical. The actual income that would be generated with this set of assumptions would vary from company to company based on differences in life expectancy tables and expenses that are in use.*

Single Life Annuity - *The annuity used in this chapter is a single life annuity, so the income covers the life of one individual and stops at death.*

AIR - *There is a 4% AIR built into the contract.*

Investment Lag - *The life annuity is assumed to be participating in the investment in real time. If this were an actual annuity product, there would be a lag between when the investment experience occurred, and when it was factored into the payment (usually the lag is a month, or a year).*

By assuming that the annuity is participating in the current year's return, we can compare it more easily to a periodic withdrawal, which is subject to real time investment returns.

The trade off is that this will slightly skew results, but any impact to a given set of results will decrease as the number of iterations increases.

Taxes – *The model does not account for taxes. It is very possible that the variable annuity income would be taxed at normal income tax rates, while the periodic withdrawal could be taxed at long term capital gains rates. This might greatly impact the results.*

Final Note – *The random returns generated by this calculator are governed by an average return and a standard deviation, and a bell curve distribution.*

Although applying random returns to a retirement income model is superior to using a flat rate of return, it is not a panacea. There are still risks in using the model since random returns are not akin to predicting future events. As well, more advanced statistical methods may be needed to create more realistic results, or mimic a particular investment which does not conform very closely to this set of parameters.

CONCLUSION

The comparative analysis in this chapter provides a significant step towards the kind of analysis needed to make the right retirement decision.

However, since different results are generated each time the calculator is run, it is very hard to draw a conclusion. We will begin to remedy this in the next chapter by recording the results.

CHAPTER SEVENTEEN QUESTIONS

1.) In the first set of results, the periodic withdrawal underperformed the annuity because:

A.) Poor returns led to asset erosion.

B.) Possibly because the model did not take into account the Annuity Income Shortfall.

C.) Both A and B.

D.) Neither A or B.

2.) In the second set of results, both income options produced large incomes. This example is not likely in reality because:

A.) Stocks have not historically produced returns this large over such a long period of time.

B.) The random return generator contains parameters for only averages and standard deviations. A more complex model would self-correct for such a long string of robust returns.

C.) Both A and B.

D.) Neither A or B.

3.) Ways to measure the performance of a life annuity include:

A.) How it compares to a periodic withdrawal when the same set of assumptions are used.

B.) How much it pays out compared to a fixed period annuity with a similar length.

C.) Both A and B.

D.) Neither A or B.`

4.) The hypothetical aspects of the life annuity used in the calculator include:

A.) Estimated life expectancies.

B.) The absence of a lag in performance.

C.) Both A and B.

D.) Neither A or B.

5.) To create a more realistic model, an actual annuity product should be researched and the following factors determined:

A.) The life expectancy used for your age and gender.

B.) The assumed interest rate.

C.) Actual operating and mortality costs.

D.) All of the above.

CHAPTER EIGHTEEN

REVIEWING RETIREMENT OUTCOMES

In the previous chapter, the **Periodic Withdrawal** and **Variable Life Annuity** were subjected to **Investment Volatility**.

Although viewing the wide range of results was helpful, it would be even more helpful if we could attribute a likelihood of success to each of them.

The calculator featured in this chapter, the **Multiple Iteration Calculator**, will move towards that solution by taking the steps of running the assumptions through the model a thousand times and plotting all of the outcomes together on a chart. Below is the set of assumptions we'll use, as well as a screenshot showing the output:

ASSUMPTIONS

Starting Age: 65
Lifespan: 100
Beginning Balance: $860,000
Annual Withdrawal: $60,000
Average Return: 7.5%
Standard Deviation: 18
Average Inflation: 2.5%
Standard Deviation: 2.5

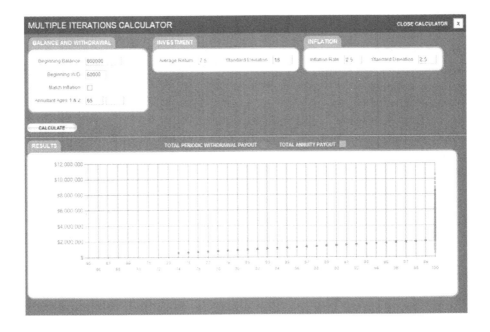

In the chart above, there are a thousand results plotted (they can't all be individually be identified due to overlapping results).

Each of these dots indicates the total amount paid out, as well as the point in time that the periodic withdrawal was terminated due to lack of funds.

They begin at age 71. Many of them are clustered at age 100, which indicates that a good portion of the time, the periodic withdrawal lasted up to the maximum age allowed by the calculator.

On the other hand, the green/lighter dots, which represent the variable life annuity, all occur at age 100. This is because the annuity will always payout for the life of the annuitant, and the calculator assumes a lifespan of 100 (By definition the income could only fall short of age 100 if the annuity company went out of business).

This view of the data provides greater insight into the range of possible incomes. But this analysis can be taken a step further by using statistical calculations to assign a probability of success associated with each outcome.

CONCLUSION

This chapter was devoted to producing and plotting one thousand outcomes on a scatter chart to shed some light on the range of possible outcomes; however, in the next chapter this will be improved upon by assigning a probability of success to each of the outcomes.

CHAPTER EIGHTEEN QUESTIONS

1.) The point of a scatter plot graph is to:

A.) Find trends by grouping together occurrences with similar values.

B.) Help estimate the most likely outcome of a scenario.

C.) Allow comparisons between two competing models.

D.) Show how changes in assumptions may affect outcomes.

E.) All of the above.

2.) When a standard deviation is not included in the assumptions, the scatter plot:

A.) Produces only 1 dot indicating that there is only one possible outcome for the scenario.

B.) The scatter plot produces a large number of dots, that may include a thick tail.

C.) Both A and B.

D.) Neither A or B.

3.) In the calculator provided in this chapter, a proper comparison cannot be made between the life annuity and the periodic withdrawal because:

A.) They are different income options.

B.) The annuity model does not take into account the Annuity Income Shortfall.

C.) The annuity income is subject to a lag in performance.

CHAPTER NINETEEN

DETERMINING THE LIKELYHOOD OF SUCCESS

This chapter introduces the process of assigning probabilities to the output from our income model. This is the final step of a three step process known as **Regression Analysis** (or Monte Carlo Analysis).

Regression analysis is helpful in answering questions such as "Should I buy an annuity or manage my own withdrawals?", "What is the probability that the income stream will last for 10, 20 or 30 years?" and "Which income option will provide the largest payout?"

OVERVIEW OF REGRESSION ANALYSIS

Regression analysis is a three step process that includes: 1) creating a model that is subject to volatility, 2) gathering and recording the output, and 3) applying statistical methods to determine the probability of success associated with each of the outcomes.

The first two steps have been covered in the preceding chapters, therefore, in this chapter we'll focus on step number three.

TOTAL AMOUNT PAID OUT

To generate probabilities associated with the total payout of an income option, we'll use the **Total Probability Payout Calculator.** This calculator can gather data associated with a thousand iterations and then perform the requisite statistical analysis.

The output for this calculator is a chart that shows probabilities along the Y-Axis, and dollar amounts along the X-Axis. While results for the Periodic Withdrawal will be depicted in blue\dark, the Variable Life Annuity will be depicted in green\lighter.

We'll use the familiar set of assumptions listed below to generate the output:

ASSUMPTIONS

Starting Age: 65
Lifespan: 100
Beginning Balance: $860,000
Annual Withdrawal: $60,000
Average Return: 7.5%
Standard Deviation: 18
Average Inflation: 2.5%
Standard Deviation: 2.5

Below is the charted output:

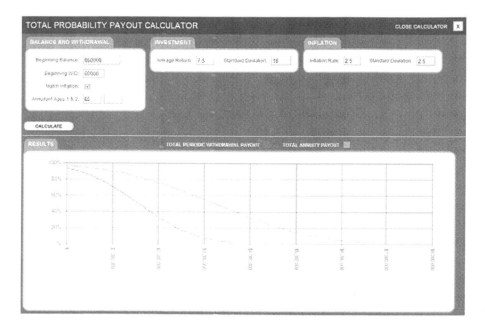

In the set of results shown, the periodic withdrawal has about a 75% chance of paying out $1,000,000, a 35% chance of paying out $2,000,000, and a 10% chance of paying out $3,000,000.

The variable life annuity, on the other hand, has about a 90% chance of paying out $1,000,000, a 75% chance of paying out $2,000,000 and a 55% chance of paying out around $3,000,000.

If this set of assumptions is re-run in the calculator, you'll notice only a slight change in the results, as opposed to the previous calculators, which generated a wider range of outcomes.

This is because the output in this calculator includes summary statistics, while in the previous calculators the results showed the underlying data.

LONGEVITY OF THE PERIODIC WITHDRAWAL

While the calculator introduced in the last section focused on the total dollars paid out, this section will introduce a calculator that measures the probabilities associated with the longevity of the periodic withdrawal.

The variable life annuity is not included in this analysis, because by definition, a variable life annuity will last for as long as the annuitant lives.

In this calculator, the Y-Axis indicates the probability of success while the X-Axis is labeled in increments of age. The assumptions are listed below:

ASSUMPTIONS

Starting Age: 65
Lifespan: 100
Beginning Balance: $860,000
Annual Withdrawal: $60,000
Average Return: 7.5%
Standard Deviation: 18
Average Inflation: 2.5%
Standard Deviation: 2.5

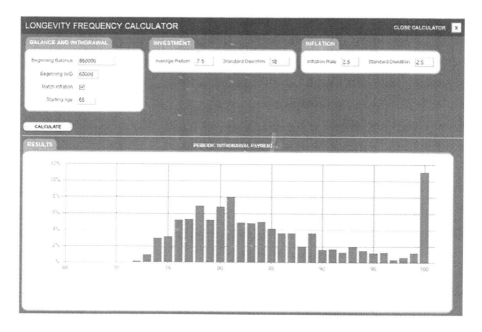

While reviewing the results in the screenshot, you'll notice that the probability of the income lasting to age 100 (for this set of assumptions) is less than 12%. The other 88% of possibilities are spread between ages 73 and 99 with the bulk of these within the range of age 75 to 85. In other words, it's much more likely that the income will terminate between the ages of 75 to 85, than that it will last to age 100.

This set of results shows the inherent risk of using a volatile investment choice to fund a periodic withdrawal. By running the calculator multiple times, you'll find that this is not an uncommon result. This risk can be reduced by using strategies that were briefly outlined in Chapter Nine.

CONCLUSION

We've covered a great deal in this volume. We've defined and described the **Periodic Withdrawal** and **Variable Life Annuity,** observed their behavior when subjected to volatility, and finally, assign probabilities of success to particular outcomes using Regression Analysis.

Through all of this, the annuity has been shown to be an attractive choice, however, there are additional considerations to take into account, and no one should make a final decision based solely on this output.

First, remember that this book closely follows only one set of assumptions. There may be other sets of assumptions in which the periodic withdrawal is more attractive. In order to experiment in this regard, we recommend that you visit www.MyRetirementLibrary.com and apply your own set of assumptions. Also, you should seek out the advice of a **Financial Planner**, and use professional grade software to run your scenarios.

Secondly, the variable annuity presented within this volume is hypothetical. The life expectancy tables and mortality expenses used to generate its results do not represent a particular variable annuity available in the marketplace. As well, the investment parameters used in this volume are based on the historical behavior of a broad stock index. There are any number of other investment choices that could be used, not to mention allocating along a number of different strategies and asset classes. You should build your own scenario around available retirement products and also determine the appropriate asset allocation appropriate for your situation.

Also, you should be aware that this analysis has not taken into account taxation, fees, or expenses that may accompany investing and receiving income. Whether you decide on a periodic withdrawal or variable life annuity, these costs will eat into your income stream and should be taken into account.

You should also consider the danger of modeling risk. For instance, the random number generator used to create our results takes into account only an average return, standard deviation, and a distribution that conforms to a standard bell curve. This model may be inadequate to mimic the behavior of the particular investment that you are considering. You should consult a financial planner that uses professional grade software and become comfortable with your understanding of the risk inherent in the model.

A short excerpt from volume two of this series on the Annuity Income Shortfall follows:

EXCERPT FROM VOLUME II:

ANNUITY INCOME SHORTFALL

The **Annuity Income Shortfall** is a phenomenon that occurs when the amount being paid out by a variable annuity falls below the amount of the initial payment (and therefore, is probably deficient to meet the budget).

An example of the Annuity Income Shortfall is found in Retirement Income Choices 101 in the first screenshot of Chapter Seventeen, which is reproduced here:

ASSUMPTIONS

Starting Age: 65
Life Span: 100
Beginning Balance: $860,000
Annual Withdrawal: $60,000
Average Return: 7.5%
Standard Deviation: 18

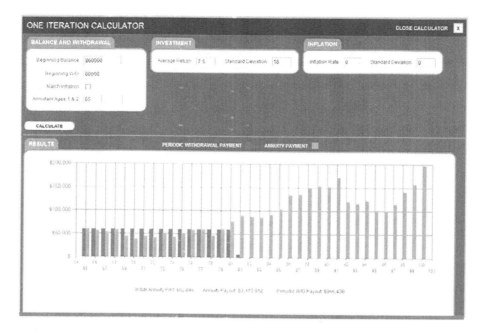

This screenshot shows the annuity income (green/light bars) falling below the initial payment of $60,000 at age 70, and not recovering until age 80. Assuming that the full $60,000 was dedicated to the retiree's fixed expenses, this would leave a shortfall, which would have to be met by other means.

ADJUSTING FOR THE ANNUITY INCOME SHORTFALL

If you commonly observe a shortfall in your retirement modeling, it's a sign that your assumptions are too aggressive. There are many methods to combat this. Although this is not an exhaustive list, they include: re-budgeting to spend a smaller amount, reinvesting in less risky assets, applying a greater number of dollars, or adjusting the model to change the investment mix.

Most of our discussion in the second volume addressing the Annuity Income Shortfall will center on incorporating a two-asset portfolio, one riskier asset, and one less risky asset. This is a

115

departure from volume one which focused on a one-asset portfolio (one risky asset).

The intent of the two-asset portfolio is to create a floor that the annuity income will not fall below. This floor will be created through the combination of the two assets. One, the less risky asset, will provide a "hard floor"—an income which will not drop below a certain level. On the other hand, there will be little or no upside potential for growth in the income associated with this asset.

The other asset (the risky asset), will provide a "soft" floor with a certain likelihood of success. In other words, there will not be a 100% certainty that the income will not fall below a certain level, but there will be a reasonable probability of success. On the other hand, the riskier asset will have more growth potential.

Through the combination of assets, we hope to lower the risk of a decrease in income, while still allowing for future growth, in order to outpace inflation.

CHAPTER NINETEEN QUESTIONS

1.) The three steps needed to perform Monte Carlo Analysis include:

A.) Creating a model that will generate observable output.

B.) Gathering the output and recording it.

C.) Performing statistical analysis on the data.

D.) Skewing the data to conform to preconceived notions.

      I.) A, B and D.

      II.) A, C and D.

      III.) A, B and C.

      IV.) A, B, C and D.

2.) Using the calculator, we can confirm that the following assumptions will lead to a smaller total income:

A.) The absence of inflation.

B.) Higher inflation.

C.) Zero volatility.

D.) Some volatility.

        I.)   B and D.

        II.)   A and D.

        III.)   C and D.

        IV.)   All of the above.

ANSWER KEY

Chapter One	1.) D	2.) A		
Chapter Two	1.) T	2.) T	3.) F	4.) T
Chapter Three	1.) D	2.) D	3.) C	
Chapter Four	1.) T	2.) T	3.) T	4.) T
Chapter Five	1.) T	2.) F	3.) T	4.) T
Chapter Six	1.) T	2.) T	3.) F	
Chapter Seven	1.) D	2.) T	3.) T	
Chapter Eight	1.) C	2.) T	3.) C	
Chapter Nine	1.) D			
Chapter Ten	1.) F			
Chapter Eleven	1.) A	2.) D		
Chapter Twelve	1.) C	2.) D		
Chapter Thirteen	1.) E	2.) A		
Chapter Fourteen	1.) C	2.) A		
Chapter Fifteen	1.) C	2.) A		
Chapter Sixteen	1.) C	2.) D		
Chapter Seventeen	1.) C	2.) C	3.) C	4.) C 5.) D
Chapter Eighteen	1.) E	2.) A	3.) B	
Chapter Nineteen	1.) III	2.) I		

INDEX

Made in the USA
Charleston, SC
02 March 2013

17823084R00072